Life Lessons
While on the Path

A guide to walking by faith

Tyra M. Ousley

ISBN: **979-8-9934-4210-5** (paperback)
ISBN: **979-8-9934-4211-2** (E-book)

For Worldwide Distribution, Printed in the U.S.A.

INTRODUCTION

There is something sacred about The Path.

Not just the physical road we walk, but the spiritual journey we each travel; the seasons of growth, the moments of stillness, the unexpected detours, and the quiet whispers of divine direction. Every step we take tells a story. Every turn holds a lesson, and every stretch of the path offers us a fresh opportunity to trust God more deeply.

Life Lessons While on the Path was born out of my own journey. One filled with questions, faith tests, breakthrough moments, and encounters with God in places I never expected. Through mountaintop joys and valley shadows, I've discovered that the path is not always easy, but it is always purposeful. Perhaps the most powerful truths are not found in reaching the destination, but in what we learn while walking.

This book is not a formula. It is not a checklist. It is a guide. It is a collection of Spirit-led reflections to help you see the hand of God in the terrain beneath your feet. Each chapter is designed to offer you wisdom, encouragement, and clarity as you walk forward, even when the road feels uncertain.

Whether you're stepping onto the path for the first time, standing at a crossroads, or pressing on after many miles, may this book serve as a companion, a voice that reminds you you're not alone and that God is with you at every point on the journey.

So, take a breath. Open your heart. Step forward.

Life Lessons are waiting While on the Path.

CONTENTS

ACKNOWLEDGMENTS

To the Author and Finisher who turned simple walks into divine revelation and birthed this book. To my husband, Keevin Ousley, who has walked with me on this journey. This is only the beginning; there is more to come, more to explore, more to be revealed. To You: Every Reader. May God meet you on your path and guide you step by step, as only He can.

1 STEPPING ONTO THE PATH

Every journey begins with a step, and not all paths are paved. Some are hidden until God reveals them. Others are already prepared, waiting for our obedience to activate the walk. The journey of faith starts not with a roadmap, but with a response, a yes to the Lord's prompting.

For me, stepping onto the path didn't happen with a grand announcement or dramatic shift. It was subtle. Quiet. It came through observation. One day, while walking, I looked up and saw people in the distance walking together, going somewhere. There was something about their movement that stirred something in my spirit. It was as if God whispered, "There's more. Follow the path."

At that moment, I realized that if I remained where I was, I would miss something. I couldn't explain it, but I knew there had to be more. We changed directions and followed the people. As we walked, a new path appeared. It was one we never knew existed. That path had always been there, but we couldn't see it until we took the first step. This is how God works. He reveals more as we obey more. It was the act of stepping forward that revealed what had been hidden.

Discoveries await those who are willing to leave the familiar. If we stay in the house, in isolation, in comfort, or in religious routine, we'll never know what's just outside our door. By the way, the "house" isn't just our home; it can be our church, our comfort zones, or our own expectations. If we refuse to venture beyond what we know, we miss divine appointments, growth opportunities, and even glimpses of God's glory.

As we walked that day, we noticed something else: people were walking, biking, and running each at their own pace. Some moved fast, others slow, while others ran circles around us. At first, I felt the urge to match their pace, until the Holy Spirit reminded me to walk at my own pace. Besides, who was I trying to impress? Those who had built up endurance could go faster; however, I was just beginning.

1

Trying to match someone else's speed will leave you breathless and behind. The goal is not speed; the goal is faithfulness. Run your race. Walk your walk at your own pace.

That day, it didn't matter how many others were around us. What mattered was that we were walking together. My husband and I, side by side. Encouraging one another and pacing one another. In marriage, you don't need a crowd; you need unity. God created the union of two for strength, companionship, and divine purpose.

On this path, there were moments of solitude. At one point, we looked back and realized the people we'd seen earlier had disappeared. It was just us and God; therefore, we kept walking.

As we continued, we heard a voice singing praises nearby. It was a sound of encouragement. It was also a reminder that we were not alone. Sometimes, as you continue on your journey, you'll hear praise before you see progress. Let those sounds lift your spirit.

We then encountered a man who passed us multiple times. Although he took a different route, we chose to stick with the path we knew, and our paths still crossed. His route wasn't wrong; it was just different. In life, some may venture off into places that feel unfamiliar to us, but in time, our paths may cross again. Stay steady.

Eventually, we came to a set of stairs which we climbed. At the top, we could see what we could never have seen from the ground. The higher you go in God, the greater your perspective. The more you press in, the more you see. Exodus 33:21 says "...there is a place by me..." says the Lord. It's a place of revelation, of clarity, of beauty and safety, that begins as you step onto the path.

Before the walk ended, we encountered a fountain; water springing up. It was a spiritual symbol. "But whoever drinks from the water that I will give him will never thirst again. In fact, the water I will give him will become a well of water springing up in him for eternal life" (John 4:14 - CSB). It was a reminder that whenever I am thirsty, whenever I need refreshing, I can drink from the fountain that never runs dry.

That first day, though rich with experience, our bodies were physically exhausted. We were just beginning our journey toward fitness. All we wanted was to make it back home and rest. As we neared the end of our walk, the sun began to shine brightly, almost as if it were beaming down directly on us. I closed my eyes, lifted my face toward the Son, and could hear Him say: "I am with you and am shining upon you." Caught up in the moment, I was smiling at Him, and He was smiling back at me. As I opened my eyes, I saw that we were approaching a gate. It felt symbolic and deeply fitting. Naturally, the gate was a marker. It symbolized that we were close to our destination. We knew then that we could not stop. We were almost there. We encouraged each other and ourselves to keep going... just a few more steps. Psalms 100:4 then echoed in my spirit: "Enter his gates with thanksgiving and his courts with praise. Give thanks to him and bless his name" (CSB). In that moment, our strength was renewed. Our hearts lifted. We weren't just encouraged by what we had physically accomplished, but by the One who had been with us, leaving reminders of His presence with every step. We then passed through the gate with praise.

This was the start. The beginning of walking a path not fully seen but divinely appointed. There is more ahead, but it starts with one obedient step.

Reflection: Beginning the Journey

What has God shown you recently that stirred your heart to move?

Are there areas of your life where you're staying "in the house" instead of venturing out in faith?

Who has God placed beside you for encouragement, support, and accountability on your path?

Are you walking at your pace or trying to match someone else's?

How can you become more aware of the spiritual "stairs" around you that are calling you to go higher?

Take a moment to ask God for the courage to step fully onto the path. Trust that each step you take, no matter how slow or unsure, is seen by Him and led by Him.

2 THE TERRAIN OF TRUST

Once we say yes to the path, we soon discover it is not always level ground. The terrain shifts. What begins as smooth pavement can turn into gravel, hills, or even steep climbs. Trust is no longer a concept; it becomes a necessity.

When you're walking with God, the path will test your footing. There may be times when it seems like everything could change at any moment, as if the ground beneath is unstable. It's in those uncertain places where trust becomes active. It's not enough to believe that God is with you; you must walk as if He truly is.

On one occasion, as my husband and I ventured farther than usual, the trail grew more narrow and the edges steeper. The wind picked up. What was once a leisurely stroll became a focused, cautious walk, but we didn't turn back. We kept walking, remembering that we had already come a long way.

Trust is remembering what God said, even when it looks like the way ahead is unclear. It's choosing to keep going even when the familiar fades away. The terrain of trust demands a deeper level of surrender.

There will be moments when it seems like God has led you into a place that doesn't make sense. You may ask, "Why am I here?" or "Did I take a wrong turn?" But in those places, God is not trying to confuse you; He is preparing you. He is building your faith muscle.

Think of Abraham. God told him to go "to the land that I will show you" (Genesis 12:1-CSB). There was no map. No visible destination. Only an instruction, and a God who promised to lead. Abraham had to walk it out, one day at a time. So must we.

Sometimes, the path gets lonely, while at other times, it gets crowded with distractions. Either way, the key is to stay focused. Look up, not around. Trust that God's path is not only good but tailored just for you.

Along the terrain of trust, you may lose things: Comfort. Control. Certainty, but what you gain is greater: Clarity, Endurance, Intimacy with God. You begin to know Him. Not just as a guide, but as your source. Just when you

4

feel like the terrain will never level out, you turn a corner and discover peace. A resting place. A breath of fresh air. That's how trust works; it leads you through the unknown to a place of assurance.

Reflection: Trusting the Ground Beneath You

What areas of your life feel unstable right now? How is God asking you to trust Him in those places?

Can you recall a time when obedience led you somewhere unfamiliar, but fruitful?

Are there areas where you're hesitating to move forward because you can't see the outcome?

What promises of God can you hold onto when the terrain of life becomes difficult?

How is God building your faith as you walk with Him?

Take a moment to breathe and surrender the need to see every step. Rest in knowing that God is the One who orders the path and walks it with you.

3 ENCOUNTERS ON THE WAY

When you choose to walk the path God has for you, you don't walk alone. Along the journey, you will encounter people, some expected, others surprising. These encounters are not random; they are divine appointments.

One morning while walking, my husband and I met a couple who commented that it would have been a good day to sleep in. As we continued walking on our own routes, it occurred to me that our paths would never have crossed if we had done that. How many encounters do we miss because we choose comfort over calling? Every individual you encounter along the way serves a purpose, be it to provide support, impart knowledge, or just to let you know you're not alone.

God uses people to speak into your journey. Sometimes it's through a kind word, a shared story, or even a moment of laughter. These divine interruptions are often the fuel you need to keep going. Hebrews 13:2 reminds us, "Don't neglect to show hospitality, for by doing this some have welcomed angels as guests without knowing it" (CSB).

Encounters, however, are not just about receiving; they are also about giving. As you walk the path, your presence can be the answer to someone else's prayer. Your smile, your hello, your testimony might be the very thing they need to keep moving.

Some encounters serve as mirrors. They reflect where you are on your journey. Some people you meet will be further along. Instead of comparing, observe. Learn. Let their endurance remind you that you, too, can go the distance.

Some people, on the other hand, appear to move in circles or even backward. These experiences serve as reminders of where you have come and the importance of staying the course. Offer grace and extend a word in season. You never know what battle someone else is fighting.

Sometimes you'll walk alongside someone for only a season. Don't be discouraged when their path deviates from yours. Not everyone is meant to stay with you. Some are assigned for a stretch of your journey, just enough to teach you something or deposit something valuable into your spirit.

Other times, you will be the one passing someone else. You may exchange nothing more than a nod or a wave. Still, those moments matter. Every encounter is a chance to reflect the light of Christ.

We also encountered people moving at different paces; some sprinting, others strolling. Everyone was headed somewhere, but not everyone was aware of the path's purpose. Some were distracted, on their phones or in their own world, unaware of what was happening around them. That reminded me: awareness matters. You can be on the path and still miss the moment.

As you walk, stay alert. Stay present. The people you meet may carry keys to your next breakthrough, or you may carry keys to theirs. Trust God with each encounter. Trust that He is orchestrating your path and the people along it.

Reflection: People Along the Path

Who has God placed on your path recently, and what might He be showing you through that connection?

Have you dismissed any encounters as random that may have been divinely orchestrated?

Are you open to being a vessel of encouragement for others along their journey?

In what ways do you tend to compare your walk to others, and how can you refocus on your own pace?

How can you stay spiritually alert and aware of the purpose in every encounter?

Take a moment to thank God for those He's placed on your path: past, present, and future. Ask Him to make you sensitive to divine appointments and to use you as a light to those you meet.

4 THE NARROW PLACES

Not every stretch of the path is wide or easy to navigate. There are narrow places. Those that are tight, constrained, uncomfortable sections of the journey where there's little room to move, little room to carry extra weight, and no room for distractions. These are the seasons where God refines us.

Matthew 7:14 says, "How narrow is the gate and difficult the road that leads to life, and few find it" (CSB). The narrow path requires intention. It demands surrender. It's not a place for the casual traveler, but for the committed journeyer.

During one of our walks, the path grew tight; overgrown brush and trees pressed in on both sides. There was only room for one person to pass at a time. In that moment, I was reminded that not everything can go with you into the narrow place. Unnecessary burdens such as fear, pride, comparison, and even people at times, must be released to continue forward.

The narrow places are often lonely. You might not see others, and you may even feel unseen yourself, but you have to know that these places are not punishment; they are preparation. These are times that push you closer to the heart of God. They cause you to rely solely on His voice, His direction, His strength.

Narrow places also quiet the noise. You're less likely to be distracted when there's no room to wander. You become more attuned to what really matters, and you hear God more clearly.

We've learned on these walks that the narrow path eventually opens again, and oftentimes, you don't come out the same way you entered. You come out lighter, stronger, sharper, and more aware.

If you're walking through a narrow place right now, don't despise it and don't rush through it. Let it do its work in you. Ask God what He's trying to prune and what He's calling you to let go of. The narrow place is where transformation happens.

It's in these tight places that perseverance is birthed, character is shaped, and purpose is clarified. When you emerge, you'll be more prepared for the wider places ahead; those open fields of purpose and impact.

The narrow places are not forever, but they are necessary.

Reflection: Embracing the Narrow Path

What burdens might God be asking you to release in this season?

How has God used narrow or difficult places to shape your character?

Are there distractions or detours you need to lay down to stay on course?

What is the Spirit highlighting in your heart during this tight stretch of your journey?

Can you see the beauty and necessity of the narrow path in your life right now?

Take a moment to thank God for the narrow places. They may not feel comfortable, but they are purposeful. Ask Him to help you walk through them with grace, endurance, and a teachable heart.

5 THE UNEXPECTED TURNS

No matter how well you think you know the path, life has a way of introducing the unexpected. These occur when detours, delays, and unforeseen circumstances arise. These things are not meant for destruction, but for development. The unexpected turns on the journey are where faith is forged, and flexibility is tested.

On one of our morning walks, we had a clear route in mind. We had taken it many times before, but this time, a portion of the path was blocked. Construction had begun, and we were forced to turn around and take another route. At first, frustration tried to settle in, but soon we realized we had just discovered a new portion of the path we hadn't known existed. The detour became a blessing.

God often redirects us, not because we're off course, but because He wants to show us more. Proverbs 16:9 says, "A person's heart plans his way, but the Lord determines his steps" (CSB). The unexpected turns may feel like interruptions, but they're divine re-directions.

Sometimes, the turns are internal emotional shifts, spiritual stretching, or changes in relationships. These turns can feel like you're veering off-track, but in God's plan, they are still part of your journey. He wastes nothing. What may appear to be a setback might actually be a setup for something greater.

While on the path, you may reach a sign that reads "Trail Ends. No Through Access," but nearby, you see another sign pointing to a newly constructed route that bypasses the blocked area. In life, one door may close, but God always provides another way forward. Our responsibility is to stay sensitive and obedient to His leading.

In these turns, we also encounter the opportunity to let go of control. Our plans may be precise, but they are limited. God's perspective sees the whole trail. Isaiah 55:8-9 reminds us that His thoughts and ways are higher than ours.

There is also a spiritual maturity that grows when we accept the turns.

Instead of panic, we learn peace. Instead of resistance, we learn release. We begin to trust that God's redirections are not detours from destiny but doorways into it.

So when the path changes, when life throws a curve, pause. Breathe. Listen. Ask, "Lord, what are you showing me here?" Let the unexpected lead you into greater expectation.

Reflection: Navigating Life's Detours

What unexpected turn in your life ended up revealing something good or necessary?

How do you typically respond when your plans are interrupted? How can you better trust God in those moments?

Are there any closed paths in your life that God is redirecting you from?

What new opportunities or perspectives have come out of a recent detour?

How can you cultivate peace and patience when the journey doesn't go as planned?

Take time today to release your need for control. Embrace the mystery of the journey, and invite God to surprise you with His better way.

6 THE ROCKY GROUND

There are places along the path that feel jagged, unstable, and uneven. These are the rocky grounds; moments in life when everything feels like an uphill climb and steady footing seems impossible. These are the trials that test not only our endurance but also our faith.

During one of our walks, we veered onto a section of pavement that was riddled with cracks and protruding stones. It wasn't pleasant. Our steps became more cautious, slower, and more deliberate, but we noticed something: we were still moving forward. The rocky places didn't stop us; they simply made us more aware.

Life will bring rocky ground in the form of seasons of financial struggle, emotional weight, relational tension, or spiritual dryness. Rocky, however, does not mean impassable. It means careful, prayerful movement is required. These are the places where we depend on God more than ever. Psalm 18:33 says, "He makes my feet like the feet of a deer and sets me securely on the heights" (CSB).

In the rocky places, we must watch our step. We can't afford to rush. A loose shoelace or a misstep can trip us up if we're distracted or burdened. We have to slow down, ask for wisdom, and walk in discernment. This is where spiritual maturity is forged, not in ease, but in endurance.

Sometimes, those jagged places are reminders that we've carried too much weight. The rocky places invite us to check what we're carrying. Are we weighed down by worry, comparison, or fear? Now is the time to lay it down.

Interestingly, we noticed that grass and even small flowers were growing up through some of the cracks. Life can still spring forth in the most broken places. God can bring beauty from the struggle.

Eventually, the rocky ground gave way to smooth pavement, but the lessons we learned in that rough terrain stayed with us. Sometimes God allows and utilizes the rocky ground not as punishment, but to develop and produce steadiness, a dependence, and a greater faith in us.

The rocky ground is not forever, but it is necessary. Keep walking. You're not stuck, you're being strengthened.

Reflection: Walking Through the Rough Places

What rocky places are you currently facing, and how have they affected your pace or posture?

What obstacles are you facing that require careful navigation to maneuver through and strength to leap over?

How has God shown up for you in your toughest seasons?

What areas have you noticed something beautiful springing up through the rocky places?

How can you encourage someone else who is navigating rocky ground?

Ask the Lord to give you grace and sure footing today. Even in hard places, He is present. Even in rough terrain, you are still on the path.

7 CONTINUAL TREADING CREATES A PATH

Not every path is paved or planned. Some are created by persistence. There are times in life when we don't find a trail already carved out for us. It's in those times that we must tread and create one ourselves.

As we walked, we noticed that there were some places where the grass had been worn down, not by machinery, but by footsteps. Someone had chosen to walk a different way, a shorter or more direct route, and over time, their consistency created a path.

This is what happens when someone dares to go where others have not. At first, the way is overgrown, hidden, and unclear, but through repeated movement and courage, that new path becomes visible not just to the one walking, but to others who pass by.

Sometimes the assigned route seems longer, more complicated. We may be tempted to create a shortcut, not out of rebellion, but through wisdom and revelation. These moments require discernment. There is a difference between forging ahead out of impatience and forging ahead by divine direction.

Abraham left everything familiar to follow God into the unknown. Hebrews 11:8 says, "By faith Abraham, when he was called, obeyed ... He went out, even though he did not know where he was going" (CSB). His steps of obedience created a path for an entire generation to follow.

If you feel like you're walking through high grass, unsure of what's ahead, but you know God is leading you, keep going. Your continual treading is doing more than getting you through. It's creating a way for someone else. Sometimes others won't see or understand why you're walking that way, but God does, and over time, that path becomes a testimony and a blueprint for others.

You may not feel like a trailblazer, but someone behind you is following your lead. Keep walking.

Reflection: Making New Paths

Where have you sensed God asking you to walk where others haven't?

Are you facing resistance because the path does not yet exist?

What steps of faith have you taken that might be paving the way for others?

How does persistence shape legacy?

In what ways can you encourage others to trust the new paths God is leading them into?

Ask the Lord to give you courage and clarity. Even if it looks like you're the first to walk this way, trust that He's gone before you, and that you are not alone.

8 OFF THE BEATEN PATH

"Off the beaten path" refers to places that are secluded, unfamiliar, and not commonly traveled. These are the places that require us to step beyond our comfort zones, venture into the unknown, and follow routes that may not make sense to others.

It is in these uncommon spaces, far from the crowd and beyond what's familiar, that God often calls us. Here, He invites us into deeper trust, radical obedience, and bold acts of faith that challenge logic and reason. But if these paths lead to such profound encounters with God, then why, among so many believers, do so few ever arrive at this sacred place of miraculous living?

The answer lies in faith. True faith, as described in Hebrews 11, is not based on prior evidence or visible proof. It's the deep, internal assurance that what we hope for will surely come to pass. "Now faith is the reality of what is hoped for..." (Hebrews 11:1- CSB).

This kind of faith doesn't wait for a blueprint. It remains steady in uncertainty and isn't shaken by present circumstances. It walks with eyes fixed solely on The One who spoke and follows Him, even into the unknown.

Examples in Scripture show what it looks like to go off the beaten path:

Ruth left her homeland to follow Naomi and embrace the God of Israel (Ruth 1:16).

Noah built an ark at God's word, trusting what he had never seen (Hebrews 11:7).

Moses obeyed God and faced Pharaoh to declare freedom for God's people.

Abraham prepared to sacrifice Isaac, fully believing God could raise him from the dead (Hebrews 11:17–19).

The three Hebrew boys set a powerful precedent for unwavering trust in God, even under the threat of a fiery death. Their bold faith not only demonstrated steadfastness but also drew God's divine intervention on their behalf (Daniel 3).

Daniel, when surrounded by predators in the lion's den, modeled a calm and unshakable faith. He showed us how to remain at rest and undisturbed, fully trusting in God's protection (Daniel 6).

This kind of faith walks in step with God, not because of what is seen, but because of who He is. It is confident in His voice, even when there is no precedent. It trusts when there is no blueprint. This is the faith that causes Jesus to marvel (Matthew 8:10).

Is going off the beaten path an invitation to believe God more boldly, to follow Him more fully, and to obey Him without hesitation?

"Everything is possible to the one who believes" (Mark 9:23- CSB). Faith that doubts will not move mountains (Mark 11:23). Faith is a sign of how the righteous live (Romans 1:17).

To go off the beaten path requires:

- Confidence in God's nature
- Obedience to His Word
- Unshakeable trust regardless of circumstance
- A willingness to be misunderstood or unseen

It is a call to unusual boldness that turns the world upside down (Acts 17:6).

This is not just a place of physical movement; it's a spiritual realm of faith that increases, matures, and expands beyond the ordinary (2 Thessalonians 1:3; Mark 2:1-12).

Reflection: Walking Where Few Tread

What "unusual" step has God asked you to take that feels off the beaten path?

How do you respond when there are no reference points except God's voice?

Which of the biblical examples resonates most with your own journey of faith?

Are you willing to be misunderstood for doing something only God told you to do?

What does great boldness in your faith look like right now?

Ask God to strengthen your faith, to help you trust Him when it doesn't make sense, and to lead you boldly down the path few dare to travel.

9 SIGNS AND WARNINGS ALONG THE WAY

While walking along the path, there are moments when warnings appear, which are posted not only to inform but to protect. Signs that say, "Stay on the path to avoid poison ivy," offer more than just practical guidance. Spiritually, these signs represent the instruction and correction we receive from God's Word to help us avoid unnecessary pain and danger.

Some signs serve as a caution. "Beware of Dog" signals potential threats, just as God often provides gentle nudges or firm instructions to warn us about people, places, or decisions that could cause harm.

There are also directional signs. These are signs that confirm we are on the right track. At times, we walk without certainty, wondering if we've made the correct turn, but as we continue in obedience, the signs begin to appear. These signs validate our path, letting us know that we are headed in the right direction.

Sometimes we'll come to a decision point: two paths lie before us. One looks riskier, like a log over a stream, narrow and dangerous. In the distance, we might spot an overpass, slightly out of the way but far safer. The spiritual parallel here is clear: some choices may seem faster or more exciting, but wisdom tells us to take the path that leads to safety and peace, even if it takes longer.

There are times on the path when the terrain seems unfamiliar, and fear begins to rise. You may feel like you've entered a dark or threatening place, but remember, God is with you. His angels guard you, His peace goes before you, and often, what looks unfamiliar turns out to be a place you've been before, just from a different angle.

Not every portion of the path will be beautiful or easy. Some areas are filled with weeds, darkness, or tension, but these places often hold people who need the Light of the world. If we don't go into those areas, how will they experience the hope we carry?

While on the path, there can be atmospheric changes. There are days when the wind is strong, temperatures drop, or rain begins to fall, but the determined walker doesn't stop. Even when no one else is out there, you keep going.

Sometimes the light drizzle turns into a full downpour, but as you press forward, you see shelter ahead. These moments remind us that there are seasons when we must pick up the pace, grow in discipline, and move forward with greater urgency. Hebrews 5:14 reminds us that maturity comes through use and practice. It's in those rain-soaked moments that our strength and discernment are exercised.

Then, there are winds of resistance. Unlike gentle breezes, these winds push against your forward motion. Spiritually, these are the trials, conflicts, or oppositions we face. When this happens, don't retreat. Lean in. Push back. Keep moving.

Even in the resistance, there are sweet moments, like catching the scent of honeysuckle or pine. These fragrances remind us of God's presence. They lift our spirits and declare that everything in creation bears witness to His goodness.

Sometimes, God directs us down a road we didn't plan to travel. We follow because we trust. The way may seem longer, unfamiliar, or uncertain, but suddenly, we get a glimpse of the destination. It's distant, but it's there, and in those moments, our hope is restored.

However, before we get there, there may be more annoyances to deal with, such as spider webs to brush off, little irritants to fan away, slick roads to negotiate, and puddles to cross. However, with each step, we gain experience, become more resilient, and grow more confident. Eventually, we get there. The journey was harder than expected, but the arrival makes it all worth it

---

Reflection: Reading the Signs

What signs has God placed in your life recently that you may have overlooked?

Have you ever chosen the log over the overpass? What did you learn?

In what ways have you experienced the winds of resistance?

What do you do when the destination feels farther away the more you walk?

How can you stay sensitive to God's direction when the path feels unclear?

Ask God to give you spiritual eyes to see His signs, a willing heart to obey, and the endurance to continue walking, especially when the path demands more than you expected.

10 LIFE LESSONS IN THE VALLEYS

Every journey has its mountaintops. Those high, victorious moments when everything seems clear and the presence of God is tangible. As certain as those moments are, we can be just as certain that every path also descends into valleys. Those low, quiet, sometimes shadowed places are often where the deepest lessons are learned.

In the valley, things slow down. The pace is no longer brisk; it's measured. The terrain may be soft from recent rains, making each step feel heavier. The valley isn't always a place of excitement. It's a place of endurance, quiet, and reflection; yet, it is sacred.

David, the shepherd king, spoke of walking "through the valley of the shadow of death" in Psalm 23. He didn't fear, not because the valley wasn't real or dangerous, but because he knew Who was with him. The valley revealed the faithfulness of God in a way the mountaintop never could.

In the valley:

We learn dependence. There is no rushing ahead. There's no pretending we have everything figured out. In the valley, we walk with open hands, learning to rely on God for daily guidance.

We develop depth. Shallow roots don't survive in dry places. The valley presses us to sink our roots deep into the truth of God's Word. It's where we grow, even if growth feels invisible at the time.

We recognize the Shepherd. In the valley, the voice of the Shepherd becomes clearer. There are fewer distractions, fewer people, and less noise.

We become attuned to His leading in the stillness.

We become prepared. Just as fruit is harvested in the valley, not on the peaks, the valley seasons prepare us to carry the weight of the blessings on the next hilltop. These are the places of equipping.

Often, valleys precede new elevations. Before promotion, there is proving. Before exaltation, there is humility, and in the depths, God shapes us for what's next.

Some valleys are long, and others are brief. Some are emotional, others spiritual. Some come with grief, loss, or deep disappointment. Others come from obedience as we are led there by God Himself for our refining.

But even in the valleys, there are hidden treasures. Isaiah 45:3 says, "I will give you the treasures of darkness and riches from secret places..." (CSB). The valley may be dark, but there are riches there: wisdom, compassion, endurance, empathy, and a deeper knowing of God's heart.

And when we emerge from the valley, we don't come out the same. We are stronger, wiser, and more secure in who God is.

Reflection: Growth in the Low Places

Have you recently experienced a valley season in your life? What did it teach you?

How did your perspective of God shift while in the valley?

What "hidden treasures" did you discover during that time?

In what ways did the valley prepare you for what came next?

How can you encourage someone else who may be walking through their own valley?

Ask the Lord to help you embrace valley seasons not as punishment, but as preparation. Trust that even in the lowest places, His presence is guiding, shaping, and sustaining you.

11 WHEN THE PATH IS CROWDED

There are moments on the path when you find yourself surrounded. The once peaceful and solitary walk becomes noisy, fast-paced, and filled with others who are also running their race. These are the crowded seasons of life; the times when community, competition, distraction, or even confusion press in close.

At first, the crowd might feel energizing because you see that you are not alone. Others are journeying, too. There's a sense of movement and momentum, but after a while, the noise can drown out your clarity. The pace of others might tempt you to speed up when you need to slow down. Their direction might cause you to question your own. In these moments, staying focused becomes essential.

Jesus understood what it meant to be surrounded. The crowds followed Him everywhere. They pressed against Him, sought something from Him, even touched Him without permission, and yet, He never lost His focus. He stayed on mission. He only did what the Father told Him to do, even when everyone else had a different expectation.

In crowded seasons:

You must guard your focus. Not every voice deserves your attention. Not every movement is yours to follow. Tune your ear to the Shepherd, not the crowd.

You must walk at your own pace. Don't rush because others are running.

You may be healing while they are sprinting. You may be listening while they are shouting. Let God set your rhythm.

You must remember your assignment. Crowds bring comparison. It's easy to look at others and feel behind, less equipped, or even unworthy, but God has called you to a specific place on the path. Stay true to it.

You must remain grounded in identity. The crowd will try to define you.

They'll label your journey or question your direction, but when your identity is rooted in Christ, you won't be shaken by outside opinions.

Even in the crowd, God sees you. Just as He saw the woman with the issue of blood, who touched the hem of Jesus's garment, He knows your need. While others press in for their own reasons, He can pick you out and call you daughter, son, beloved.

There will also be times when the crowded path means community. People who walk with you, support you, challenge you, and encourage you. These moments are precious and necessary. Iron sharpens iron, and the Body of Christ thrives when it moves in unity, but even then, your walk with God is personal. You must be able to hear His voice above the crowd.

Reflection: Moving with Purpose in Crowded Spaces

Are you in a season where your path feels crowded? What are the main distractions or pressures you're facing?

How can you refocus your heart and mind to stay aligned with God's voice?

Are you tempted to compare your journey to others around you? What truth from God's Word can anchor you in your unique calling?

In what ways can community be a gift rather than a hindrance on your path?

What intentional boundaries or disciplines do you need to put in place to maintain clarity?

Ask God to help you walk confidently and peacefully, even when the path is full. May you remain sensitive to His voice, anchored in His Word, and secure in your identity.

12 WHEN THE HIDDEN STRENGTH IS STILLNESS

There are moments on the journey where forward motion seems to stop. The path levels out, the scenery stills, and there is no wind pushing you ahead. These are the moments of stillness. Not pause for rest, not delay from distraction, but intentional stillness, divinely orchestrated by God.

Oftentimes, it can feel unnatural. We live in a world that glorifies constant activity, quick results, and loud proclamations, but God's ways are not our ways. Sometimes, the most powerful thing we can do is wait, be quiet, and trust Him in the silence.

Psalm 46:10 commands, "Be still, and know that I am God..." Stillness brings awareness. It strips away distractions. It sharpens our hearing. It tunes our hearts, and in it, God whispers reminders of who He is and who we are in Him.

Stillness doesn't mean stagnation. It is a space where strength is cultivated. Isaiah 30:15 says, "... in quietness and in confidence shall be your strength..." These are sacred moments on the path when God calls you to simply be with Him, in Him, and before Him.

In stillness:

God strengthens your spirit. While others may seem to be passing you by, He is fortifying your foundation for the next season.

God recalibrates your focus. The clarity you need doesn't always come in motion; it often arrives in silence.

God heals your soul. Stillness is often the soil where restoration grows. Wounds, griefs, and weariness are tended to in the quiet.

God prepares your next steps. Stillness is not a sign of delay; it is the incubation chamber of divine direction.

Even Jesus withdrew to solitary places. He embraced stillness to commune

24

with the Father, not because He lacked power, but because He desired alignment.

If the journey has slowed, don't resist it. Don't panic. Don't strive. Instead, settle in. Be still. Receive. Listen. Allow the hidden strength of stillness to shape you from the inside out.

Reflection: Leaning into the Quiet

Are you currently in a season of stillness or silence? How do you feel about it?

What do you think God might be teaching or developing in you during this time?

Are there areas of your life that need realignment, and could stillness be the way God is guiding you back?

What are some practical ways you can quiet your soul and intentionally sit in God's presence?

How has stillness helped you grow in your faith in the past?

Invite God to meet you in the quiet places. Let Him renew your strength, deepen your trust, and reveal His heart in the stillness.

13 DETOURS & DIVINE REROUTES

Not every journey is linear. On the path of life, we often expect straight roads and predictable progress, but God often leads us by way of detours, unexpected shifts that reroute us from where we thought we were going.

At first, detours can feel like disruptions. They seem to delay our progress or distance us from our destination. We wonder: Did I make a wrong turn? Did I miss God's voice? Why is this taking so long? But in God's hands, detours are not distractions; they are divine strategies.

Consider the Israelites after they left Egypt. Exodus 13:17-18 tells us that God did not lead them through the shortest route, though it was nearer. Instead, He led them the long way around. God said, "The people will change their minds and return to Egypt if they face war" (CSB). God rerouted them to protect them and prepare them.

Sometimes the road we would choose isn't the one that will shape us. Sometimes, God takes us around what we thought we were ready for, to preserve us for what we're truly called to.

Detours serve a purpose:

They protect us from dangers we cannot see. We may think we're ready, but God knows what lies ahead and reroutes us for our good.

They build our faith. When we don't understand why or how long, we learn to trust God's timing over our own.

They change our perspective. The alternate route often gives us a new view of God, ourselves, and the journey itself.

They introduce us to divine appointments. On detours, we often meet people or encounter situations that shift our destiny, like Ruth in the field of Boaz, or the Samaritan woman at the well.

They prepare us for what's next. God uses longer routes to strengthen our character and deepen our dependency on Him.

There are also times when we're headed in the wrong direction, not because God led us there, but because of our own choices. Even when we veer off course, God, in His mercy, graciously reroutes us and realigns us with His path. That's why Proverbs 3:5-6 reminds us not to rely on our understanding, but to acknowledge God in all our ways, so that He can guide our steps.

Even delays caused by our own choices do not cancel God's plan. Just like a GPS recalculates when we miss a turn, the Holy Spirit gently redirects us. God never wastes time, even when it feels like time is lost.

Reflection: Trusting the Longer Way

Have you experienced a recent detour in your life or faith journey? How did you respond?

What has God revealed to you in seasons where the path was different than expected?

Are there situations where you need to release control and trust God's rerouting?

How have unexpected paths led to unexpected blessings in your life?

What might God be preparing you for right now, through the scenic route?

Invite the Lord to show you the purpose of every turn. Trust that even when the path changes, His promises remain. He is a faithful guide, and every reroute in His hands leads somewhere meaningful.

14 THE POWER OF PERSPECTIVE

The path we walk rarely changes as much as our view of it does. Perspective encompasses both the way we perceive and what we view. It is possible for two people to walk the same road and have very different experiences. One sees obstacles, the other sees opportunities. One sees delays, the other sees divine timing. One sees barren land; the other sees soil prepared for growth.

What makes the difference? Perspective.

God often invites us to come up higher to see things from His vantage point. In Revelation 4:1, John was told, "Come up here, and I will show you..." (CSB) A shift in elevation always brings a shift in understanding. What seems overwhelming from the ground looks small from above.

Perspective is shaped by:

What you believe about God. Do you trust that He is sovereign, wise, and good even when life doesn't feel like it? Your view of God shapes your view of everything else.

What you've been through. Sometimes, past pain can cloud present perception. Other times, past victories anchor us in faith.

What voices you listen to. The voices you allow in your life: people, media, even internal dialogue, can lift your perspective or weigh it down.

Where you fix your focus. Are your eyes on the problem or the promise? The mountain or the One who moves mountains?

Paul said in 2 Corinthians 4:18, "So we do not focus on what is seen, but on what is unseen. For what is seen is temporary, but what is unseen is eternal" (CSB). That's the essence of a kingdom perspective, seeing with eyes of faith, not just natural sight.

When we walk the path with the right perspective:

We stop comparing our pace with others. We understand that God uniquely designs each person's path.

We are less shaken by setbacks, and we begin to recognize that detours and delays often carry hidden blessings.

We are more grateful. When our eyes are open to what God is doing, even in the hard places, we cultivate a spirit of thanksgiving.

We become hope carriers. Others around us are encouraged when we choose to see the good, speak faith, and remain steady in uncertainty.

The enemy often attacks perspective first. If he can distort how you see, he can derail how you walk; however, when we keep our eyes fixed on Jesus, the Author and Finisher of our faith, clarity returns.

Reflection: Seeing From the Viewpoint of Heaven

How has your perspective shaped your current journey, whether positively or negatively?

What areas in your life need a shift in how you see them?

Are there situations where you've focused more on what you lack than on what God has promised?

How can you train your mind and spirit to respond with faith, not fear?

What would it look like today to view your path the way God sees it?

Pray for divine perspective. Ask God to help you rise above the noise, the fear, and the temporary, so that you can walk with confidence and clarity. When your perspective aligns with His promises, your steps will follow with faith.

15 CROSSING THE FINISH LINE

Every path has a purpose, and every race has a finish line. No one begins a journey simply to wander forever. There's a destination in mind, a place God has prepared not just around you but within you. While there are many lessons, valleys, detours, and victories along the way, the end of the path brings something sacred: fulfillment.

Paul understood this. As he approached the end of his race, he declared in 2 Timothy 4:7, "I have fought a good fight, I have finished my course, I have kept the faith." His words ring with finality, but also with victory. Not because everything had been easy, but because he had endured. He had stayed on course, trusted God, and finished strong. Finishing well isn't about perfection; it's about perseverance.

On this path:

You will get tired, but Isaiah 40:31 promises that those who wait on the Lord will renew their strength.

You will be tempted to quit, but Galatians 6:9 is a reminder not to grow weary in doing good, for in due season, we shall reap if we faint not.

You will sometimes feel alone, but you're never truly alone. Jesus walks every mile with you, and His Spirit empowers you to endure.

You will experience both joy and pain, but Romans 8:28 assures us that all things, yes, ALL, are working together for your good.

When you near the end of a journey, you often reflect. You see how far you've come, what you've overcome, and what God has done. The rocky places, the winds of resistance, the detours, the quiet valleys; they all lead to this place.

Crossing the finish line means:

You trusted God even when the path didn't make sense.

You kept moving even when it hurt.

You stayed faithful even when few understood your journey.

You lived a life that pointed others to Him.

Jesus, too, crossed His finish line. On the cross, He spoke the words: "It is finished." (John 19:30) That wasn't defeat, it was victory. It was completion. It was obedience fulfilled.

The same can be said for those who endure: it is not about fame, applause, or even ease, but about faithful obedience to what God assigned. Your finish line may not be marked with fanfare. It may not look like anyone else's, but it is significant, and it is seen and applauded by Heaven, and when you cross it, there's a reward, an eternal one.

"Well done, good and faithful servant... enter thou into the joy of thy Lord." Matthew 25:23

Reflection: Finishing with Faith

What does "finishing well" look like for you in this season of your life?

Are there areas where you've been tempted to stop or settle short of the finish line?

What helps you stay focused when the journey is long?

Who has modeled finishing well in your life, and what can you learn from them?

How can you encourage others to stay the course and finish strong?

This chapter marks a closing, but not the end. In God's kingdom, every finish line becomes a new beginning. May you walk faithfully, run purposefully, and finish joyfully.

BONUS SECTION: DEVOTIONAL JOURNAL

Space of Reflection, Prayer, and Application

May this Journal be a tool for prayer, reflection, and transformation

This Devotional Journal was created to accompany you on your journey.

As you read Life Lessons While on the Path, I hope that it uncovered deep truths and spiritual insights that resonated with your personal journey. Some lessons, however, require more than reading; they require reflection. This Devotional Journal invites you to slow down, engage your heart, and meet God in a deeper way.

Each entry is designed to help you pause and process what the Holy Spirit may be highlighting along your path. The questions and prompts following every chapter are not simply for answering; they are for listening, discovering, and growing. They are spaces to wrestle and worship, to be honest and still, to bring your thoughts before the Lord and allow Him to speak to them.

Whether you use this journal as part of a morning quiet time, an evening wind-down, or a midweek check-in, may it become a sacred space where your pen becomes a prayer, and your words echo your faith in motion.

Let this be more than a journal. Let it be a place of encounter.

The Path is still unfolding, but God is always guiding.

Chapter 1 – Stepping Onto the Path

Scripture Meditation
"… This is the way. Walk in it." (Isaiah 30:21)

Ask: What does taking that first step into God's path feel like for me?

_____
_____
_____
_____
_____

Personal Reflection

When did I sense God inviting me to leave comfort and begin walking?

_____
_____
_____
_____
_____

What fears or doubts did I experience, and how did I respond?

_____
_____
_____
_____
_____

Prayer Focus
"Lord, help me boldly walk the steps You've called me to. Not by sight but by faith."

Next Step
Identify a small first move you can make this week to follow God's call (a new habit, prayer time, act of service).

_____

_____

_____

_____

_____

Stillness with God
Sit in silence and listen to any invitation He's placing on your heart.

My Response

Use this space to capture your thoughts, prayers, or any insights God highlighted as you reflected on this chapter. Write freely and revisit as the Holy Spirit continues to speak.

_____

_____

_____

_____

_____

_____

Faith Responses

In this section, write down the ways your faith has been stretched or strengthened through this chapter. Record prayers, questions, or moments of growth you want to remember.

_____

_____

_____

_____

_____

_____

Heart Responses

Take time to pour out what's on your heart. Express gratitude, wrestle with questions, or note areas where God is inviting you into deeper trust.

_____

_____

_____

_____

_____

_____

_____

NOTES

Chapter 2 – The Terrain of Trust

Scripture Meditation
"How happy is anyone who has put his trust in the Lord…" (Psalm 40:4)

Ask: Where do I need to choose faith before I feel clarity?

_____
_____
_____
_____
_____

Personal Reflection

What confusing or winding season am I currently walking through?

_____
_____
_____
_____
_____

How have I seen God's Word guide me when paths felt unclear?

_____
_____
_____
_____
_____

Prayer Focus
"Father, teach me to trust You in each curve, even when I can't see the destination."

Next Step
Pick a verse to memorize or post in a visible place as a trust anchor.

_____
_____
_____
_____
_____

Stillness with God
Be still and notice any specific insights He gives about trusting Him now.

My Response

Use this space to capture your thoughts, prayers, or any insights God highlighted as you reflected on this chapter. Write freely and revisit as the Holy Spirit continues to speak.

_____
_____
_____
_____
_____
_____
_____

Faith Responses

In this section, write down the ways your faith has been stretched or strengthened through this chapter. Record prayers, questions, or moments of growth you want to remember.

_____
_____
_____
_____
_____
_____
_____

Heart Responses

Take time to pour out what's on your heart. Express gratitude, wrestle with questions, or note areas where God is inviting you into deeper trust.

_____

_____

_____

_____

_____

_____

_____

NOTES

Chapter 3 – Encounters on the Way

Scripture Meditation
"Don't neglect to show hospitality…" (Hebrews 13:2)

Ask: Which divine appointment has stood out in my journey?

_____
_____
_____
_____
_____

Personal Reflection

Recall someone God placed on your path and describe what their presence meant.

_____
_____
_____
_____
_____

What might He want you to say or do for someone coming into your life now?

_____
_____
_____
_____
_____

Prayer Focus
"Lord, open my eyes to see Your appointments and give me a heart to respond in love."

Next Step
Reach out to someone God has highlighted. Send a message, pray, or offer help.

_____
_____
_____
_____
_____

Stillness with God
Quietly listen: Is there someone you feel nudged to connect with?

My Response

Use this space to capture your thoughts, prayers, or any insights God highlighted as you reflected on this chapter. Write freely and revisit as the Holy Spirit continues to speak.

_____
_____
_____
_____
_____
_____

Faith Responses

In this section, write down the ways your faith has been stretched or strengthened through this chapter. Record prayers, questions, or moments of growth you want to remember.

_____
_____
_____
_____
_____
_____

Heart Responses

Take time to pour out what's on your heart. Express gratitude, wrestle with questions, or note areas where God is inviting you into deeper trust.

_____

_____

_____

_____

_____

_____

_____

NOTES

Chapter 4 – The Narrow Places

Scripture Meditation
"Strait is the gate, and narrow is the way..." (Matthew 7:14)

Ask: What narrow season am I experiencing, and what is it shaping me for?

_____
_____
_____
_____
_____

Personal Reflection

How has a season of restrictions or limits refined my character?

_____
_____
_____
_____
_____

Where am I tempted to step off into a wider, easier route?

_____
_____
_____
_____
_____

Prayer Focus
"Jesus, grant me grace to remain in the narrow even when wide roads entice me."

Next Step
Devise a plan to release something God has instructed you to give up.

_____
_____
_____
_____
_____

Stillness with God
Pause and allow Him to speak courage into your narrow place.

My Response

Use this space to capture your thoughts, prayers, or any insights God highlighted as you reflected on this chapter. Write freely and revisit as the Holy Spirit continues to speak.

_____
_____
_____
_____
_____
_____
_____

Faith Responses

In this section, write down the ways your faith has been stretched or strengthened through this chapter. Record prayers, questions, or moments of growth you want to remember.

_____
_____
_____
_____
_____
_____
_____

Heart Responses

Take time to pour out what's on your heart. Express gratitude, wrestle with questions, or note areas where God is inviting you into deeper trust.

_____

_____

_____

_____

_____

_____

_____

NOTES

Chapter 5 – The Unexpected Turns

Scripture Meditation
"A man's heart plans his way, but the Lord directs his steps." (Proverbs 16:9)

Ask: How has God's redirection surprised me and turned out good?

_____
_____
_____
_____
_____

Personal Reflection

When did a divine reroute bring blessing or insight?

_____
_____
_____
_____
_____

What direction am I resisting or fearing today?

_____
_____
_____
_____
_____

Prayer Focus
"Father, align my heart with Yours. Help me yield to Your reroutes without fear."

Next Step
List any upcoming decisions and ask God for confirmation through prayer.

_____
_____
_____
_____
_____

Stillness with God
Sit quietly and sense His peace in your current season of change.

My Response

Use this space to capture your thoughts, prayers, or any insights God highlighted as you reflected on this chapter. Write freely and revisit as the Holy Spirit continues to speak.

_____
_____
_____
_____
_____
_____
_____

Faith Responses

In this section, write down the ways your faith has been stretched or strengthened through this chapter. Record prayers, questions, or moments of growth you want to remember.

_____
_____
_____
_____
_____
_____
_____

Heart Responses

Take time to pour out what's on your heart. Express gratitude, wrestle with questions, or note areas where God is inviting you into deeper trust.

_____

_____

_____

_____

_____

_____

_____

NOTES

Chapter 6 – The Rocky Ground

Scripture Meditation
"He makes my feet like the feet of a deer…" (Psalm 18:33)

_____

Ask: In what rocky place am I growing faith and stamina?

_____
_____
_____
_____
_____

Personal Reflection

How have difficult seasons strengthened rather than derailed me?

_____
_____
_____
_____
_____

What thorn or obstacle am I learning to leap over?

_____
_____
_____
_____
_____

Prayer Focus
"God, let this rocky terrain cultivate deeper dependency on You and stronger faith in me."

Next Step
Identify one practical way to persevere through current difficulties (scripture, rest, community).

_____
_____
_____
_____
_____

Stillness with God
Rest in His presence and sense His support beneath your feet.

My Response

Use this space to capture your thoughts, prayers, or any insights God highlighted as you reflected on this chapter. Write freely and revisit as the Holy Spirit continues to speak.

_____
_____
_____
_____
_____
_____

Faith Responses

In this section, write down the ways your faith has been stretched or strengthened through this chapter. Record prayers, questions, or moments of growth you want to remember.

_____
_____
_____
_____
_____
_____

Heart Responses

Take time to pour out what's on your heart. Express gratitude, wrestle with questions, or note areas where God is inviting you into deeper trust.

_____

_____

_____

_____

_____

_____

_____

NOTES

Chapter 7 – Continual Treading Creates a Path

Scripture Meditation
"By faith... Noah... prepared... by faith Abraham... obeyed..." (Hebrews 11)

Ask: What small step am I taking now that could pave a new path?

_____

_____

_____

_____

_____

Personal Reflection

How has your steady obedience opened doors or created new space?

_____

_____

_____

_____

_____

Where might God be calling you to step into something uncharted?

_____

_____

_____

_____

_____

Prayer Focus
"Lord, give me courage to begin, even where no path is visible, to pioneer with faith."

Next Step
Choose one new act of faith to repeat daily for the next week.

_____

_____

_____

_____

_____

Stillness with God
Listen for His encouragement in your small steps toward obedience.

My Response

Use this space to capture your thoughts, prayers, or any insights God highlighted as you reflected on this chapter. Write freely and revisit as the Holy Spirit continues to speak.

_____

_____

_____

_____

_____

_____

_____

Faith Responses

In this section, write down the ways your faith has been stretched or strengthened through this chapter. Record prayers, questions, or moments of growth you want to remember.

_____

_____

_____

_____

_____

_____

_____

Heart Responses

Take time to pour out what's on your heart. Express gratitude, wrestle with questions, or note areas where God is inviting you into deeper trust.

_____

_____

_____

_____

_____

_____

_____

NOTES

Chapter 8 – Off the Beaten Path

Scripture Meditation
"Faith is the assurance of things hoped for …" (Hebrews 11:1)

Ask: Where is God inviting me to believe beyond what I can see?

_____

_____

_____

_____

_____

Personal Reflection

When was I called to follow God outside the familiar?

_____

_____

_____

_____

_____

How have I responded when asked to take the road less traveled?

_____

_____

_____

_____

_____

Prayer Focus
"God, give me boldness to walk by faith, even when the way is unusual and unpopular."

Next Step
Identify one "faith risk" you've been hesitating to take, write it down, and begin to pray into it.

_____
_____
_____
_____
_____

Stillness with God
Ask the Lord to increase your faith and show you what's possible when you obey.

My Response

Use this space to capture your thoughts, prayers, or any insights God highlighted as you reflected on this chapter. Write freely and revisit as the Holy Spirit continues to speak.

_____
_____
_____
_____
_____
_____
_____

Faith Responses

In this section, write down the ways your faith has been stretched or strengthened through this chapter. Record prayers, questions, or moments of growth you want to remember.

_____
_____
_____
_____
_____
_____
_____

Heart Responses

Take time to pour out what's on your heart. Express gratitude, wrestle with
questions, or note areas where God is inviting you into deeper trust.

_____
_____
_____
_____
_____
_____
_____

NOTES

Chapter 9 – Signs and Warnings Along the Way

Scripture Meditation
"Your word is a lamp to my feet and a light to my path." (Psalm 119:105)

Ask: What warning or direction has God recently given me?

_____

_____

_____

_____

_____

Personal Reflection

Have I been sensitive to God's signs or ignored His guidance?

_____

_____

_____

_____

_____

What signs or cautions do I need to honor in this season?

_____

_____

_____

_____

_____

Prayer Focus
"Holy Spirit, help me notice the signs You place before me. Teach me to discern and respond."

Next Step
Pay attention this week to one warning or prompt God gives you and obey quickly.

_____

_____

_____

_____

_____

Stillness with God
Invite Him to show you where He may be redirecting you or asking you to pause.

My Response

Use this space to capture your thoughts, prayers, or any insights God highlighted as you reflected on this chapter. Write freely and revisit as the Holy Spirit continues to speak.

_____

_____

_____

_____

_____

_____

_____

Faith Responses

In this section, write down the ways your faith has been stretched or strengthened through this chapter. Record prayers, questions, or moments of growth you want to remember.

_____

_____

_____

_____

_____

_____

_____

Heart Responses

Take time to pour out what's on your heart. Express gratitude, wrestle with questions, or note areas where God is inviting you into deeper trust.

_____

_____

_____

_____

_____

_____

_____

NOTES

Chapter 10 – Life Lessons in the Valleys

Scripture Meditation
"Yea, though I walk through the valley… I will fear no evil: for thou art with me." (Psalm 23:4)

Ask: How is God forming me in the valley?

_____

_____

_____

_____

_____

Personal Reflection

What has this valley season taught me about myself and about God?

_____

_____

_____

_____

_____

How has God met me in quiet, hidden places?

_____

_____

_____

_____

_____

Prayer Focus
"Lord, I choose to embrace this valley as a place of growth, not defeat."

Next Step
Journal three things God has done in the valley that you couldn't have learned on the mountaintop.

_____

_____

_____

_____

_____

Stillness with God
Sit in gratitude for His presence with you in the quiet places.

My Response

Use this space to capture your thoughts, prayers, or any insights God highlighted as you reflected on this chapter. Write freely and revisit as the Holy Spirit continues to speak.

_____

_____

_____

_____

_____

_____

_____

Faith Responses

In this section, write down the ways your faith has been stretched or strengthened through this chapter. Record prayers, questions, or moments of growth you want to remember.

_____

_____

_____

_____

_____

_____

_____

Heart Responses

Take time to pour out what's on your heart. Express gratitude, wrestle with questions, or note areas where God is inviting you into deeper trust.

_____
_____
_____
_____
_____
_____
_____

NOTES

Chapter 11 – When the Path Is Crowded

Scripture Meditation
"Let us run with endurance the race that is set before us, looking unto Jesus…" (Hebrews 12:1–2)

Ask: What distracts me when the path gets noisy or busy?

_____
_____
_____
_____
_____

Personal Reflection

How do I stay focused on my own journey when surrounded by others?

_____
_____
_____
_____
_____

What voices or expectations do I need to silence?

_____
_____
_____
_____
_____

Prayer Focus
"Jesus, be my focus. Help me run my race and not be distracted by the crowd."

Next Step
Write out your personal mission or calling and reflect on it when you feel pulled by comparison or noise.

_____
_____
_____
_____
_____

Stillness with God
Invite Him to speak clarity over your assignment and renew your focus.

My Response

Use this space to capture your thoughts, prayers, or any insights God highlighted as you reflected on this chapter. Write freely and revisit as the Holy Spirit continues to speak.

_____
_____
_____
_____
_____
_____

Faith Responses

In this section, write down the ways your faith has been stretched or strengthened through this chapter. Record prayers, questions, or moments of growth you want to remember.

_____
_____
_____
_____
_____
_____

Heart Responses

Take time to pour out what's on your heart. Express gratitude, wrestle with questions, or note areas where God is inviting you into deeper trust.

_____

_____

_____

_____

_____

_____

_____

NOTES

Chapter 12 – The Hidden Strength of Stillness

Scripture Meditation
"In quietness and confidence shall be your strength." (Isaiah 30:15)

Ask: What season am I in, and what pace is God setting?

_____
_____
_____
_____
_____

Personal Reflection

Am I rushing what God wants to slow, or am I dragging behind what He wants to accelerate?

_____
_____
_____
_____
_____

How can I better match His rhythm?

_____
_____
_____
_____
_____

Prayer Focus
"Lord, teach me to walk in step with Your Spirit; neither ahead nor behind."

Next Step
Create space this week to either slow down or speed up, whichever God is prompting.

_____
_____
_____
_____
_____

Stillness with God
Rest and ask Him to show you how He's working in this current pace.

My Response

Use this space to capture your thoughts, prayers, or any insights God highlighted as you reflected on this chapter. Write freely and revisit as the Holy Spirit continues to speak.

_____
_____
_____
_____
_____
_____

Faith Responses

In this section, write down the ways your faith has been stretched or strengthened through this chapter. Record prayers, questions, or moments of growth you want to remember.

_____
_____
_____
_____
_____
_____

Heart Responses

Take time to pour out what's on your heart. Express gratitude, wrestle with questions, or note areas where God is inviting you into deeper trust.

_____
_____
_____
_____
_____
_____
_____

NOTES

Chapter 13 – Detours and Divine Reroutes

Scripture Meditation
"For my thoughts are not your thoughts, neither are your ways my ways…"
(Is 55:8)

Ask: Are there areas of my life where I still feel uncertain or delayed?

_____
_____
_____
_____
_____

Personal Reflection

In hindsight, has a past detour protected or prepared you in ways you couldn't
see at the time?

_____
_____
_____
_____
_____

Can you identify a "divine appointment" that only happened because of an
unexpected turn?

_____
_____
_____
_____
_____

Prayer Focus
"Holy Spirit, show me what expectations I need to surrender so that God's
rerouting can be fully embraced."

Next Step

Ask God to order your steps this week and be intentional in following where He leads.

_____
_____
_____
_____
_____

Stillness with God

Reflect on how you have been able to see God differently as a result of a divine reroute.

My Response

Use this space to capture your thoughts, prayers, or any insights God highlighted as you reflected on this chapter. Write freely and revisit as the Holy Spirit continues to speak.

_____
_____
_____
_____
_____
_____
_____

Faith Responses

In this section, write down the ways your faith has been stretched or strengthened through this chapter. Record prayers, questions, or moments of growth you want to remember.

_____
_____
_____
_____
_____
_____
_____

Heart Responses

Take time to pour out what's on your heart. Express gratitude, wrestle with questions, or note areas where God is inviting you into deeper trust.

_____

_____

_____

_____

_____

_____

_____

NOTES

Chapter 14 – The Power of Perspective

Scripture Meditation
"We fix our eyes on not what is seen, but on what is unseen..." (2 Corinthians 4:18)

Ask: Are there areas of my life where comparison has skewed my vision?

_____

_____

_____

_____

_____

Personal Reflection

How would my current situation look different if I viewed it from God's perspective?

_____

_____

_____

_____

_____

Is my focus more on what's lacking, or on how God is present in the midst of it?

_____

_____

_____

_____

_____

Prayer Focus
"Holy Spirit, help me to see with eyes of faith and eternal purpose."

Next Step
Write down areas where your perspective needs realignment.

_____

_____

_____

_____

_____

Stillness with God
Father, help me to see as You see. Help me walk with clarity, peace, and bold vision.

My Response

Use this space to capture your thoughts, prayers, or any insights God highlighted as you reflected on this chapter. Write freely and revisit as the Holy Spirit continues to speak.

_____

_____

_____

_____

_____

_____

_____

Faith Responses

In this section, write down the ways your faith has been stretched or strengthened through this chapter. Record prayers, questions, or moments of growth you want to remember.

_____

_____

_____

_____

_____

_____

_____

Heart Responses

Take time to pour out what's on your heart. Express gratitude, wrestle with questions, or note areas where God is inviting you into deeper trust.

_____

_____

_____

_____

_____

_____

_____

NOTES

Chapter 15 – Crossing the Finish Line

Scripture Meditation
"I have fought the good fight, I have finished the race, I have kept the faith."
(2 Timothy 4:7)

Ask: What does finishing well look like in this season of my life?

_____
_____
_____
_____
_____

Personal Reflection

How can I stay faithful even in the mundane or unnoticed moments?

_____
_____
_____
_____
_____

What legacy do I want to leave on the path?

_____
_____
_____
_____
_____

Prayer Focus
"Jesus, strengthen my resolve to finish well and let my life echo faithfulness to You."

Next Step
Write a personal "finish strong" prayer or declaration for your current
assignment or season.

_____

_____

_____

_____

_____

Stillness with God
Imagine Him at the finish line cheering you on. Receive His joy over your
journey.

My Response

Use this space to capture your thoughts, prayers, or any insights God
highlighted as you reflected on this chapter. Write freely and revisit as the
Holy Spirit continues to speak.

_____

_____

_____

_____

_____

_____

_____

Faith Responses

In this section, write down the ways your faith has been stretched or
strengthened through this chapter. Record prayers, questions, or moments of
growth you want to remember.

_____

_____

_____

_____

_____

_____

_____

Heart Responses

Take time to pour out what's on your heart. Express gratitude, wrestle with questions, or note areas where God is inviting you into deeper trust.

_____

_____

_____

_____

_____

_____

_____

NOTES

ABOUT THE AUTHOR

Tyra M. Ousley is a faith writer, counselor, speaker, and encourager dedicated to helping others walk in purpose, identity, and deep trust in God. With a heart for spiritual growth and genuine connection, she shares biblical truths through life lessons, honest reflections, and practical encouragement. Tyra and her husband serve as community leaders, creating spaces of hope and hospitality. When she's not writing, you'll find her mentoring others, praying with them, or hosting conversations that draw people closer to God.